Two by Two

Adapted by Kate Ruttle and Richard Brown
Illustrated by David Parkins

CAMBRIDGE
UNIVERSITY PRESS

Mr and Mrs Noah built an ark.

3

The animals went in two by two,

the elephant and the kangaroo.

The animals went in three by three,

the wasp, the ant and the bumblebee.

The animals went in four by four,

the great hippopotamus stuck in the door.

The animals went in five by five,

they took some food to keep them alive.

The animals went in six by six,

the kangaroos laughed at the monkeys' tricks.

They all went into the ark

because it was starting to rain.

Mr and Mrs Noah built an ark.
The animals went in two by two,
the elephant and the kangaroo.
The animals went in three by three,
the wasp, the ant and the bumblebee.
The animals went in four by four,
the great hippopotamus stuck in the door.
The animals went in five by five,
they took some food to keep them alive.
The animals went in six by six,
the kangaroos laughed at the monkeys' tricks.
They all went into the ark
because it was starting to rain.